when they say

you can't go home again,

what they mean is

you were never there

Also by Marty McConnell

wine for a shotgun

Gathering Voices: Creating a Community-Based Workshop

when they say
you can't go home again,
what they mean is
you were never there

Marty McConnell

Winner of the 2017 Michael Waters Poetry Prize

Published by the University of Southern Indiana
Evansville, Indiana

ISBN: 978-1-930508-42-2   First Edition

Printed in the USA
Library of Congress Control Number: 2018953882

This publication is made possible by the support of the Indiana Arts Commission, the National Endowment for the Arts, the Vanderburgh Community Foundation, the University of Southern Indiana College of Liberal Arts, the USI Department of English, the USI Foundation, and the USI Society for Arts & Humanities.

Southern Indiana Review Press
Orr Center #2009
University of Southern Indiana
8600 University Boulevard
Evansville, Indiana 47712

sir.press@usi.edu
usi.edu/sir
Ron Mitchell & Marcus Wicker, eds.

Cover art: *witness*; © 2017 Lindsey Dorr-Niro; *lindseydorrniro.com*
Cover design: Matthew McNerney
Layout: Megan Miller

contents

come now, let's sit in what light is left   1

fuse   3

love in the Late Holocene   4

apocalypse lipstick   5

West Barry Street   9

notes on the warranted strife to come   11

supplication with grimy windowpane   12

when the time comes to be happy, you will be happy   13

radio silence, WENZ, WJMO, Cleveland   14

the sacrament of penance   16

the sacrament of hope after despair   17

the admiral   18

white girl interrogates her unreliable memory of certain eras   19

elegy instructions   20

this world is going to end and it's going to be fucking beautiful   23

meet me at the end of the world—I'll be the one in sequins   28

February   31

white girl interrogates her recurring dreams   32

white girl interrogates the Oklahoma bill banning the wearing of hoodies   34

queerer weather   36

Isla Vista   37

lucky   38

the reckoning   40

the sacrament of penance also has four parts   42

treatise on the nature of non-abandonment   45

white girl interrogates her own heart again   48

July, when we didn't burn the city down   49

watershed   55

our joke   56

a thing   57

I mean   58

honestly   59

not   60

things we could be if we are not us   61

distance indicated by degrees of blue   62

in the dim,   63

beloved   64

the sacrament of holding hands   67

when they say you can't go home again, what they mean is you
    were never there   68

disasterology: how to survive the apocalypse   70

how   71

actual rapture   72

•

acknowledgments   75

Eternity is always already now.

−Ken Wilber

come now, let's sit in what light is left

Out here I can believe
this world isn't going to end
or not yet. Or not

here, that the painter
in the garden harvesting the last
spring kale, the giant white dog

gentling against the blue
house, the clamor of chickens
and this sweetly

creaking tree swing will go on
and on, so even as riots and ocean
consume all the lilacs

but these, some bright
impenetrable sphere
will form around this now

of the blooming hostas
and wind ruffling the pine
branches, the high-up

dialogue of starlings
as evening's April chill
strolls in. I know

this world is going
to end, I feel it
in the concrete

and guttering light.
But there is
a yellow chair

here, facing the trees,
and I will sit in it and ask you
to come closer, to bring

yard violets and sweetgrass
to burn and ask you
once again to forget.

fuse

In the photograph I do not have of us
we are lying on a mattress in an otherwise

vacant apartment. It's clear from the angle
that one of us has taken the shot, the way lovers do

in moments of happiness, to preserve
something of it or to show off to their friends

or just to know what they look like, lying there,
before anything's exploded.

love in the Late Holocene

Since the beginning of time it's gotten hotter and hotter and now, just when I'm beginning to get comfortable, it's all starting to stop. Boys with flashlights and folded tents approaching. You say *the beginning of time* and mean a theory about planets. I mean I mean, something about humans being molecules mashed together whether they like it or not. Some watches must be worn to stay wound. Our kitchen clock is one hour and every day a few more seconds behind thanks to daylight savings, batteries invented to go obsolete, and our laziness or unwillingness to pull over a chair. Once, in the middle of a storm, tornado sirens blaring, some men the next camp site over tried to help us take down our canopy and tent. Cell phones for flashlights, and your headlamp through the rain. In the morning, a twisted giraffe of metal testified to our shared failure. It's not that I want to be alone, more that this human suit is so molecularly dense and prone to sadness. Lights moving through a ripe field. Some cold encroaching fog.

apocalypse lipstick

How shall we pretty for this ruin? Day into day
the core fails, the words dissemble, the flowers
push their gaud faces up through the crushing
season. Fuck it. Let's costume the dissolution
with brilliance. Let's train ourselves
like the slow slow dying to see

only light. Only the dim slumped sun
gushing into the next busted eon.
Take the ordinary raw from my mouth,
the gummy meat of this flaccid tongue.
Bring on the garbled bargainers of Wall Street

and State. Here are my very best boots. Here
is my weeping in the corner of the old tea shop.
It feels so late. Here where the moon's out
all through the day. Here where opus is not
being dead yet. So late in the early

of the death century. So combustible, these
minutes, this language of sticks and baubles.
Bloom! Fake that the dust is confetti and not
shredded bone. Join the dialogue
of zeroes. Our painted mouth-holes. Code

and the constant siren lullaby. The half-life
of gunpowder is forever. Half that if it's caught
on film. Half that if the revolver's PD-issue.
Half that fired into Black. Half that fired
into space where men would be if we rubbed
our feet against the floor until lightning

starred. The sun's a gun in the maw
of the planet, all of us clocks now
showing how late late the hour,
how horror-gorgeous. All the sparks
lighting the midday dark, our faces
constant as plastics. Marked

by what we cherished. An unlatched zoo
of prophets whistling through
our tooth-holes. Can you hear me,
back across the wretched decades,
the broken cosmos? I want to say

we are still here. That a man
feeds his lover in the train station
remainder and it's still a spell against
the nothing. Our children are altars,
but also we call them flowers. Once
we were monsters. Once we were
human. Once we flew.

West Barry Street

I love the ordinary doingness
of things, the man in an olive
green jacket putting a shovel

into the trunk of his clean
gray car, leaving it open.
The redhead hustling

across the street, the stroller
in front of her bumping
over the curb, the white dog

roped to the playground fence
facing the other direction. Coming
back, the man puts in a folding

chair, another, a woman
joins him, her tan jacket
flapping, she zips it, they drive

away. Someone jogs past
as if it were her natural pace,
without effort or strain. Why

a shovel? It was red. Headphones
are getting larger again, as are strollers.
My best friend's cat had one ear

removed entirely, and it doesn't seem
to notice or mind. My astrologer says
sometimes you burn enough karma to get

a pass life, an easy ride. Last night
our neighbors to the east
had a party, the stoop abuzz

in stilettos without coats, and I thought
of going over in my house clothes
to say hello and offer blankets

or tea, but they didn't seem
to be feeling the cold. I went back
to my work and texting

with a friend whose wife made
a terrible mistake, the noise
from the party a backdrop

of garbled babble and laughter,
wind against the windows,
the occasional casualty of glass.

notes on the warranted strife to come

My white heart sits at a distance from itself hearing
the news, murder on murder. Starlings
drop from an iron sky, harbingers
of no war I want to consider. But this

is the alphabet of death: a glyph, boy
in frieze. His sister, handcuffed mid-keen
and tossed. Unholstered men considering
a body. What matters? Organ music

in the distance. Greek chorus
protests tragedy, tragedy, tragedy,
tragedy, tragedy, tragedy, tragedy. Blood
for real. Every uniform's a costume

which is a clever way of saying
I am not a murderer, though my skin
is. Until there was a word for blue
humans could not see it. Not

to blame language but let's admit
we can't hate what we can't name.
Man, playground, gun, waist
band. Boy, swing set. Heart

at a distance from itself. Sky
turning iron, storm
blue. Without a stage, tragedy
is news. Blood for real. Guns

and a sky so black with starlings
it could pass for sorrow's army's
proving ground. Circling, their eyes,
though we can't see them, seeing red.

supplication with grimy windowpane

I don't know what I'm supposed to do about the lost.
I sweep and sweep. The taxes are put away, and the hats
stacked brim to brim. The rubber ball on the radiator

just sits there. I'm alive, I'm sorry, I'm not sorry.
In the bath, my body is massive: thighs, big toes, every
pointy hair. We're out of wine. Remember when the water

was a sanctuary? Come closer now. This is the part
where I tell you what's behind the glass to which
I've pressed my entire body, pink

from the bath; this is the part where you tell me how many
of your teeth are dead, where you left the cowboy
hat you pinched from the head of your sister's

outgrown doll. It's quiet here now. Give me something
I can chew on, long into the evening. An architecture
for this salt house. This bony, birdless pen.

when the time comes to be happy, you will be happy

You will show all your teeth to the door
and it will open like the hole in your mother
through which you disgraced the air
for the first time. Everything's going to be

just fine. Your fingerprints on file
nowhere, the cases against you
thin as cheap sheets, the kind that scratch
and then shred in the dryer. It's not your
fault. But if you think the song is about

you, then it is. Lying to someone you pay
to believe you is worse than lying
to your mother. I know a man who
after his mother died, the loss

sending him into a crack abyss,
paid hookers to come to his ravaged
hotel rooms and listen to him cry.
I know. I too thought it only happened
in movies. This is an example

of how weird things can get
when we try to be happy
through other people's bodies.
In movies, whenever someone

slams the door on an alien, managing
to shut it just in time to sever
the tentacle that had reached inside,
the close-up shot on the sheared-off
member twitching on the floor means

the battle isn't over. The battle isn't over
until everybody knows who the bad guy
is. Everybody's got a role to play here.
Somebody's got to go down singing.

radio silence, WENZ, WJMO, Cleveland

I start down the road but I'm the road. Or
the stripes on the road. White. Edge-
indicative. A professor says, the history
of American music is Black history. He says it

to get a rise out of us but it's true. Or might be
as true as anything. He's teaching poetry
to a room of grad students paying
out the nose for degrees their parents
and other practical people know

to be without use. A road is practical.
Stoplights, guard rails, signage
regarding the merging of lanes:
practical. As a kid I learned

about the safety on a gun. A red button
pushed to keep it from firing. I learned
on a BB gun. For killing bats
in the family cabin. I presume
all guns have safeties, but I don't know

a lot about them. I know it's easier
to aim when you're afraid. I know
how fear rises up from the knees, how it runs
up through the gut into the hands. I started

down this road and now I'm the road so
here: a man waited 1.5 seconds
to shoot a Black boy playing
with a toy gun. The man
was a white man. Police

man. The boy was 12, was Tamir, is
dead. The history of guns is a history
of safeties. I start down the road
but I'm the gun. I start

down the road but I'm the person
on the phone calling 911. I say it
to get a rise out of me. I say something
about safeties. Something about
Tamir's sister tried to run to him

but was tackled and handcuffed
while he bled out from the gut
on the playground. It's important
to say this. It is a thing my people

did. The term *paying out the nose*
has its origins in a Danish law
whereby delinquent taxpayers
were punished by having
their noses slit. It's history. In an area

with a history of avalanches, signs
are posted: Falling Rock. In an area
with a history of murder, streets are named
after assassinated Black leaders. When I say

a history of murder, I do not mean music
though white men love murder ballads.
I do not mean music though frat boys
use Lil Wayne lyrics as an excuse
to say the N-word in public. Years ago

a man told me the history of American music
is Black history, and I believed him.
Turn it up now, whatever station it is.
I don't know how to end this.

the sacrament of penance

I come to claim the white boy who yesterday slaughtered nine Black worshippers at prayer. Because to deny him is to deny the ways he and I are the same, deny the hideous lineage that dogs us and feeds us. Gavel and spit. Rope and bumper and chain. I claim him but will not say his name. It slips down my throat like half-gone milk, slick and hard.

I come to claim the white father who gave his white boy a gun for turning 21. I claim him as my own dripping shadow, as my own burning sanctuary. I claim him with his wife, I put their names in a bucket and fill it with tar. I fill it with bleach. I fill it with salt and light it on fire. I put my name in there too, but always it comes back to me. Covered in asphalt. Covered in newsprint. Covered in grief.

I come to claim my gods who are your God who are all the winds that rise in arcing rage at what is taken, at what is taken, at what is never returned. I say wind but mean gale. I say gale but mean storm. I say storm but mean bloodsquall, I mean what is brewing will boil. It will bitter. It will burn, and burn, and these white tears kerosene on the blaze.

the sacrament of hope after despair

How many men must we survive? The fortysomething at the screen door when I was 15. Roses on the porch whenever Dad was out of town. The one who tried to rape me. The other one who tried to rape me. The one who lied and dissolved and lied and dissolved and lied until I left, then followed me home to lie again. The one who made me and broke my mother's heart. The ones with the perfect syllables concealing machetes. Getting hard pursuing ruin. The ones with the gun racks and sweet guitars. The ones rolling promotions in their suit pant pockets like loose change. The ones who lisp Audre Lorde quotes over top-shelf bourbon as if the beds they rose from to come here aren't full of women who used to have hands. Not all men, but enough. Enough.

> Oh my nephews. Oh my godson.
> You do not have to be women
> to be kind. Look at your fathers, wounded
> by their own fathering, how they make
> tea and hold you. Destroying
> nothing. Killing no one.

the admiral

Every bomber is a suicide bomber. I walked into this strip club set
to detonate. By the time the dancer leans into my ear to declare
herself *100% gay*, the second boy who blew up the marathon has

bled out on the boat or been arrested. I stopped listening to the radio
at *cornered*. I stopped apologizing for not wanting a lap dance after
the fourth naked offer. When the world's on fire, everybody finds

their own way to the water. The manicured pubes of the ladies on
stage humping the laminate with practiced indifference has all the
sex appeal of street signs or furniture assembly manuals. I expected

a room packed with wolves, slavering and grabbish. I walked into a
fishbowl of dead-faced men paying cash money to be lied to, poorly.
I left the radio on in the car, the voices of reporters filling the interior

with second-hand blood, wounds head to toe. I do not check my
phone. If any of these women offers to kiss me, I will take out my
tongue, the thing I sell to stay alive, leave it on the stage next to

the singles and the fog machine, somebody's discarded juice
glass, calling the name tattooed across one's lower back: *Serenity.*
Serenity. Whatever fluorescent god we can pay to grant it or rent it.

Holy water is made by the passing over of sanctified hands. Melted
ice at the bottom of a glass, a young killer's blood on a boat, no
saints in this country, not in this century or this joint, not the

cops nor the boy nor the bomb nor me nor the woman tucking my
torn-out tongue in her garter like a dollar bill, like a blessing, like
the end of the fairy tale, the newscast, the amen, the amen, the end.

white girl interrogates her unreliable memory of certain eras

For how many years did I sleep with that Black man in Brooklyn?
Wasn't it not-love, then love? Didn't my skin fluoresce down Malcolm
X Boulevard? Purple hair, plaid wool pants, how often did the man in
camouflage on the pay phone nod and say *You be safe now?*
Brownstone windows chunking shut, Kennedy Chicken paper bags
rustling on the stoops, rats chewing boxes for the grease, reggaeton
pulsing as car doors opened and shut. Was I straight then, or
what? Is what matters the fact that nobody was aiming
for me? How often did the cops stop me to ask if I
was lost? How long before artist lofts and Starbucks and elaborate
doughnuts and three-hundred-dollar baby strollers? Why did the one
Chinese food place that delivered never have change
for a twenty? Did a man on the boulevard try to sell me one
Q-tip, never used? Did I keep walking? Fluorescent?
Would the man I was coming to love turn out a liar
and devastating scandal? In the eight blocks between Utica and Madison
when again and again that year I did not die or come close did the
dude on the pay phone drop the dialogue to a nod? Did I leave
the apartment in the morning alone, the sun over the basketball court
and laundromat and bulletproof plastic fried chicken emporium blinding
bright? The kids on the stoops calling one another by names?

elegy instructions

We love who we can love, and the rest
stay ghosts. I can't remember
now if the dead become angels

in the popular mythology, or if we just
rise up like soap bubbles in the cold
and go. There is space in my bones

for only so much grief. The rest
has to wait for sleep, when the long
and recent lost can reach back

to pull my braided hair or sing
like they never did. All the candles
burning down to the metal, the radiator

singing its dumb water song. Let's bomb
this matchbox playground, this salted garden.
What's there to stop us but the dirt

wearing our names. A first
communion skirt. The dust
in my lungs. Knock it

out of me. Say the dead do not come back
ever. Say we earn our missionary pass
every time we kiss. What country

is this? Whose shoes
am I wearing? When
did it get so cold?

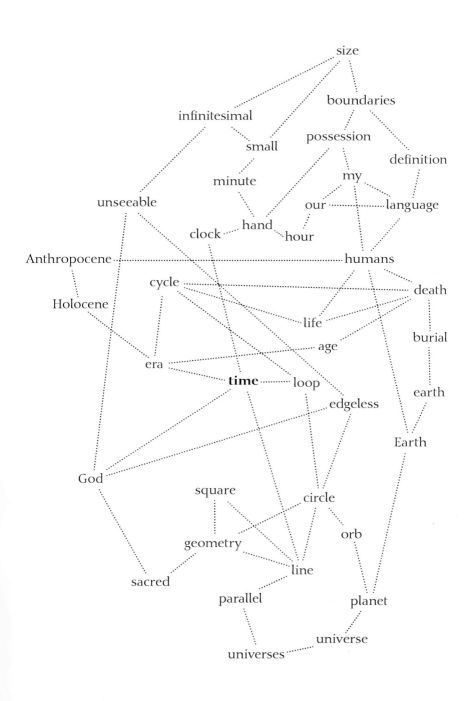

this world is going to end and it's going to be fucking beautiful

Hold me now while everything sets. I wanted to write the story
of two humans at the edge of it, their grasping for each other
and also the end of lawnmowers, how the streetlights stopped
and everywhere, even in our cities, people

could see the stars. I imagine a piano here, a man
bent over, using both hands. I'm so sad when I think
of everything ending. To be gone, to know I will be gone, is one
thing, but everything—I love how we are because it is everything

I know. Tupperware and houseplants, matching socks
and good old cheese where parts have crystallized and other parts
remain soft. All the new prodigies, the kindergartners
with their Chopin and equations—terrifying. Evolutionary.

Do you remember the night we lay on the pier and you explained
how everything changes 365 trillion times per second, remember
how the stars spread their arms though it might have been
the wine, the good, chill wood under our backs? I wanted

to write about the planet after us, but something
would not have it. On the stereo, too loud, a man
playing the piano strings with a mallet. Half
inside the lid, on loop the chorus we heard him play

at Thalia after our throat chakras burst open
and I hallucinated sound as light as strings across the ceiling
peeling back, letting us know where we came from, where
we're bound, how very star we are.

•

How very star we are. How dust-born.

We've each signed up for the mortuary parade,
that much is clear. In every tongue, death

is a door. Someone walks into a room,
someone puts on unflattering pants, the

end. Sometimes we come back. Sometimes
we hear the harps and passionate soliloquies

of the living who love us, for whom death
ignites a kind of passionate clarinet solo,

opalescent and just above ordinary. The tenor
of this, roofs above houses we didn't

even know we were living in.

•

Houses we didn't even know we were living in
shudder and tumble. For example: the weather,
and predictable seasons. The Great

Blizzard of July '35, yesterday's hurricane
and today, the sun like an anvil overheated
overhead. I'm no scientist, just a girl on a lawn

watching the moons at midday. But listen
now: we're whispering into the death
century. Sipping our way to oblivion

like a slow drunk who'll be here all
night, the shitty tipper drinking bottom-
shelf whiskey and taking up the sweetest

corner seat like nobody else needs
to get off their feet for a while. Or
we'll live forever again.

●

We'll live forever again
which is to say, until anything
that can remember
is dead. If we understand

the space between ocean and sand
as being nothing, infinitely able
to be broken down, then we know

time ghosts around us in all
directions. We know forward is
behind, and clocks
are conveniences like

stoplights, markers that keep us
from ruining each other immediately
in our big machines. If I tell you

this world is going
to end, where do you know it
to be true? I tell you
it's beautiful. It was. It will be.

•

It's beautiful. It was. It will be
but not again. A hybrid is not one thing
or another, nor are we. You know this

in your godplaces. We call
ourselves, the sun's crest and trough,
the solids and livings around us

by words, as a way
to survive our being here
together, though the crest

and trough are one—nothing
without the other. Still the words give us
apple, surface and flesh and seed and tree

and photosynthesis and fuel in our bodies
so we can wake and walk and say
our names. I call you *you*, and make a space

for you by saying it. I say *survive*
and invent for myself a place we call
later, where we are, where we are

together. It's true. You seem
the sort who'll survive.

meet me at the end of the world—I'll be the one in sequins

You seem the sort who'll survive. Whose grandfather built a bomb shelter
in the '50s and remembered to include a can opener. It's not bombs
that end us, but shelter is nonetheless essential. The light

will be that heroic twilight light that makes everything
look like a movie, like the best movie you've ever seen is just
beginning, the light that reminds you it's nearly time to come

inside, your mother waiting in an apron or the suitcase
packed or good wine chilling and the radiator beginning
to clink. Bring your instrument. While I'm waiting

I'll go over the less sad songs I have by heart.
What we did to get here is gone now, let's not talk
about it anymore. We may not need

to talk at all. You'll know me by how the light strikes
the sequins. I'll practice the cruel songs too, lying here
in the passing light. Studying the leaves

on the topmost branches on the tree at the end
of the world. We know what we did
to get here. We're still living in these mouths.

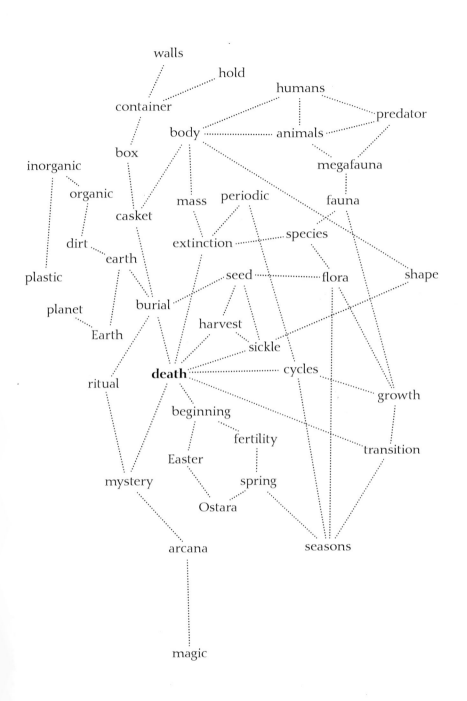

walls

hold

humans

container

predator

body

animals

box

megafauna

inorganic

organic

mass   periodic

fauna

casket

species

dirt

extinction

earth

seed   flora   shape

plastic

planet   burial

harvest

Earth

sickle

death   cycles

ritual

growth

beginning

fertility

transition

Easter

mystery   spring

Ostara

arcana   seasons

magic

February

and now the path to the house is frozen, still
winter, still winter, now the boots lined up
by the door, salt on the edges, salt
up the back side, the path to the house dirt
and ice now, the frothing snow melted

or iced hard over, no fair drifting, no gauzed treetops,
all the cars drop tires in the potholes, ice
in berms along the curbs where we stop
our cars for the night, all lined up crooked

as first teeth, facing now the streetlight, now
the front yard, ice in a ridgeback all
down the alley, ice on the dumpster, ice
on the front stoop, salt on the coat
hem, salt on the pant cuff, still winter, still

winter, frozen keyhole, lost right mitten, broken
zipper, wind between the buildings, wind between
boot strings, wind in the inch between scarf
and skin, still the machines send

the heat, still the water in the bathtub
foams, the banjo resting its strings in the corner,
roses dry on the bookshelf, a small dog slipping

across the lawn, gray and white
from the window and the wind, the wind
sliding along the building, some kind of human sin.

white girl interrogates her recurring dreams

Bone garden, bone grove, bone farm, padlock
on both church doors. Speech

upon speech on the TV, sirens and the chatter
of blackbirds on cold wires. My love

is far away from me wearing a knit
hat. A man and woman I adore

are our only way to safety. I see
no boys being killed but am aware

that they are being killed and there's
a bucket in my hands that keeps

filling and filling, getting heavier
and heavier but never overflowing, just

filling. With what? My love is way
over there. We can see each other

but not touch. I know sooner
or later she will come over

here, I know it's not for always
but this bucket. Full of ghost

bones, full of speeches, those boys
fraying pieces of hail on the marble rim

of the birdbath, over there, in the bone
garden. Starlings, starlings

in the bone farm. Then there is
a train. On it, I am aware

of my whiteness in contrast
to the other passengers and stand closer

to my friends, their brownness a comfort
I am embarrassed to feel. Where

are we going? The church
in which we find ourselves

has rooms inside of rooms. Still
I have this bucket. It is the circumference

of my hips. My love is in another part
of the house, I feel her living with the left

side of my head. Black boys
are dying, I say, dying

I say but I don't have any mouth,
just this bucket. Just this bucket.

white girl interrogates the Oklahoma bill banning the wearing of hoodies

Illegal the wearing of, but not the possession? Legal to keep
in the closet, but off the body? Or off the body outdoors
only? Behind doors, walls, windows, blinds, in the dark,
hoodie comes harmless? Stroll hallways hoodied, but not
the sidewalk? Any pavement? Any hood? Any
body? As gendered, also raced? 1957 raid

resulting in the arrest of twelve women for *mannish
dress*. Three-piece rule: at least three pieces of gender-
appropriate clothing. Body as locus of (other) control.
Body as locus of making. My sister clipped the strings
of her toddler son's so he couldn't on accident
strangle. Hoodie the staple of genderless-

ness. Hoodie the hat always on hand. Hoodie
against the Chicago gale. The Florida night. Who
gets to? Whose fine? A tithe to whom? A layer
between the head and God, layer between head
and heavens, pullover or zip, stringed or stringless,
logoed or logoless, school hoodie, fleece hoodie, black

cashmere hoodie my best friend lent me and I lost
in a breakup move. Sorry. Cashmere. Black. Fine me
for my cashmere. For my boiled wool. For my American
Apparel. $500. What else? Grommets. Strings. Shadows,
streetlights. Garter and stocking. Brassiere. Girdle
and pass. Trespass or trespass against, terrified man

with ready weapon. Steady aim. What shadow? What
beneath? What unsnatched, what unseen? Hoodie
(in)visibility. Hoodie (noun) also *hoody*, slang shortening
of hooded sweatshirt, attested by 1991. Earlier
was a familiar term for a hooded crow. What
hood? Clitoral? Executioner's? Crow's? Little Red

Riding's? Oven? Dom's? Convertible's? Mount?
How $500? How decided? How de-coded? My pale
nephew? My cashmere, lost? If not
this, what then when we rise, a murder
of hooded crows? What then against the cold?

queerer weather

Language itself inverts, subjugates, and this means
we don't have to go home alone anymore. This
is a chair that folds out into a palm tree
and I can't stand Los Angeles. Language
is the locus of all tyranny. Also, love
offered like water, the mouth giving and giving
before coming to silence, before saying
I could gift you all the noise in this body
and still the door wouldn't close. This chair
doesn't turn into anything and it's
my favorite. It's a chair. You
were born in California and that's
OK. I love you, it's true,
and people shout about it
on the television with some
frequency. They think we
and our kind will usher in a new era
which could be called *The Tyranny*
of Choice, and then their grandchildren
will marry dogs or potted plants and there goes
the family tree, so to speak. The language
of fear is magnetic and simple, easily digested
and attracted to itself. We see it
every day. This is Chicago.
The water makes the weather.

Isla Vista

the radio

my ghost

the wall

the punch bowl

staring

say the word

one time

a man took

I was not

across the street

here I am

a swarm of

hunted like

disappeared in

everybody

it's happening

I brought my ghost to the party and nobody noticed. Here I am at the punch bowl. The wall before me in pieces. Everybody's staring now. We know what has to be done. The radio tells us every day. Girls disappeared in their school skirts. Girls hunted like rabbits. There's a gun in that guy's pocket. He's not happy to see us. Here I am in pieces. The wall before me in the punch bowl. Everybody dance now. Everybody dance now. It's as though you can't say the word *rape* in a poem now without it being a rape poem. Even though it's happening. Right here in the punch bowl. I didn't have a school uniform. Also I was not raped or kidnapped at gunpoint. One time, a man took his family hostage in a house across the street from Forest Elementary. We watched the police cars from the windows or the playground, a swarm of pigtails at the edge of the gravel. They knew where to find us. They closed the school and let me walk home.

lucky

for the last dude who asked why I'm so angry

How lucky am I to have been
less drunk

> than the boy above me
> on the flowered couch
> in that dirty fraternity room. How lucky

this bucking knee, his doughy center
folding. Who was I then, to walk
down the stairs, leave by the front door, go home
to another drink. Did I tell

even my roommate? There's so much   I don't remember.

It was April. I was ten. There was a boy who kept threatening to
kiss me. I remember he had one arm on each side of my head
and I said *Don't* and he leaned in so close and said *You better
learn how to take a joke.* Then he left me alone. Let's be clear: I
wanted him to like me. Also, I was terrified. What I mean to
say is, toddlers in mascara. Kegstands on emptied stomachs.

Months after the letters started arriving from our neighbor,
full of photocopied yearbook pages, long passages in Latin,
drawings of nooses with directions, I would lie there in that
bed I had been a girl in, inventing things to say that might keep
him from killing me. What astonishes me

is not that I have survived,
but that I have not come closer   to dying.

I know the distance between me and most doors.
If you have noticed me across a room, I have already seen you looking.
And I'm   lucky.   I'm the girl who got by

unscathed. Which is to say   unpenetrated.

My beloved inherits a body that does not have to be solved.   Lucky.
My parents shut their phones off at night knowing I will not need
to be saved.   Lucky.   My debt, my frantic

laughter, my failed engagements—all my own.

When the man trapped me in that Austin hotel room, I got
out from underneath him by pretending I had to piss and
making the bathroom a barricade. You're not smarter than
me. Sometimes while making dinner or eggs, I put my hand
right next to the flame. Sometimes I take the alley, or the too-
late train. Fuck you for staring. What I mean to say is, maybe
somebody didn't raise you right. What I mean to say is, I'm sure
you're a really

nice guy. I didn't mean
what I said about your mother.
I'm sure she tried.

the reckoning

It will not be warm. It will be slow, it will be
everything. It will come with kittens in its mouth
as kindling. It will not be soft. It will call you
from the years you forgot. It will not kneel,
will not bleed, you will not see it walking but feel
its approach when the light
shrinks, when tonight's lover sighs
in her sleep, exhaling gin and vague
permissions. It will wear the face
of the men who trained you. It will have
your cruel aunt's hands. It is not a matter
of belief. It is the strictest abacus, the great scale
dangling from the hand of the woman
with the city of wind on her head. It will not ask
for consent. It will take all you have
to offer, and you will not say no.
And you will not say yes, either.

>>

And you will not say yes, either,
to offer, and you will not say no.
For consent, it will take all you have
with the city of wind on her head. It will not ask
dangling from the hand of the woman
of belief. It is the strictest abacus, the great scale,
your cruel aunt's hands. It is not a matter
of the men who trained you. It will have
permissions. It will wear the face
in her sleep, exhaling gin and vague
shrinks, when tonight's lover sighs
its approach. When the light
will not bleed, you will not see it walking but feel
from the years you forgot. It will not kneel
as kindling. It will not be soft. It will call you
everything. It will come with kittens in its mouth.
It will not be warm. It will be slow, it will be.

<<

Your cruel aunt's hands. It is not a matter
with the city of wind on her head. It will not ask,
will not bleed, you will not see it walking but feel
to offer, and you will not say no.
Shrink, when tonight's lover sighs
permissions. It will wear the face
of the men who trained you. It will have
belief. It is the strictest abacus, the great scale.
Its approach when the light
will not be warm. It will be slow, it will be
in her sleep, exhaling gin and vague
from the years you forgot. It will not kneel
for consent. It will take all you have.
Everything. It will come with kittens in its mouth,
dangling from the hand of the woman
as kindling. It will not be soft. It will call you
and you will not say yes, either.

the sacrament of penance also has four parts

1

Everything is burning and needs to. The news is not new but terrible. I pull four cards for the fate of the world: The Tower, The Hermit, 8 of Cups, 9 of Rods. This country is not the world, but it is. Structure Fire, Light in the Darkness, Walk Away from Comfort into the Unknown, Choose One Magic and Use It.

2

A brief text about the end of the world: we're it.

3

The Tower. The fate of the building, the fate of the people, the fate of the people below them waiting to catch or kill or be fallen upon like fruit by flies or a boot but wait. Who is falling, who is fallen upon? Who is the fire, who the fired upon, who in the penthouse drinking something cool counting minutes until pale angels come to save him again?

4

The Hermit. Look within, genius. Any fire worth its tinder begins at the navel. In many ways, nothing has changed. We could enter the self and never leave. We could enter the leaves, burning, and never self. Nature isn't the enemy, not even human nature. The enemy is the friend of someone who fears you enough to kill you, fears you more than regret or the inevitable loss of his inborn humanness. That person too is the enemy, but fear more his friend. Look within, genius. Whose friend. Whose enemy. The only thing that makes that lantern useful is fire.

5

Sometimes the dream of apocalypse is a copout.

6

The Hermit. You can leave the body but it won't leave you. You can leave a country but the country hits back. You can grip a city so tight all the bullets fall out but then you wake up. You can dream the apocalypse and running trains and dark noons but the news is still the news and you are still you. What're you going to do with that body now?

7

Apocalypse would be a good excuse for this paralysis. I'm always late for the protest and by late I mean I don't make it. Really good at vigils though. Practiced at holding still, holding signs, defusing the urge to weep.

8

Get it, copout? Cop a feel, cop a plea, etcetera.

White paralysis is a copout. Typing *love and light* is a copout. Staying quiet when the dude at the bar goes on about how nobody better tell him what words he gets to use, the N-word among them, says it and says it, is a copout. How badly I want to apologize to all my Black friends is a copout. But I'm sorry. I am sorry.

9

8 of Cups. For anything new to emerge, something's got to burn. But here it's all water and walking away. All our beautiful things on fire or underwater. Pick a cup and swim in it until it tips or you drown. Pick a cup and drink from it until sunflowers draw their petals back to reveal just the dark center which is like that shadow on my grandmother's tongue where what she thinks about our Black President lives. Pick a cup and sink. Pick a cup, a good one, gold or engraved and leave it by the side of the road under the overpass where people go to sleep and I lock the doors as I drive by.

10

9 of Rods. Thunder has no hands. Do you understand?

If the nature of the rod is weapon and the pacifist's song is strangled by a plastic jailhouse trash bag and the man in the penthouse sips whiskey from a snifter of exotic ice, if the nature of sunflowers is to reveal and go to seed but the four-handed girl with eight faces knows me, knows my spiny fruit heart, for what will I place the pale angel who loves me in the middle of the road? For whom cut off her wings, of them make what shade?

*

Four cards in the dark:
tinder for a world awaiting
its purifying burn.

treatise on the nature of non-abandonment

Anything can happen next. Tea, gunshots, the streetlights
          coming on outside this room, or the other, where you
                    are, with your body so like my body but with its own

          particulars, the breasts I have called *perfect*
          and the waist I tug toward me all day, listening for the one
note we produce when the city night slants across us

because someone forgot to pull the curtain
          entirely shut. I admit

          I imagined you. Despite this, your knees
are real, and your face that I say I love

          because I do, and the sound of you turning the pages
          of some large magazine full of art displayed in rooms
in countries you visited before I knew you, before
                    I even imagined you. Now

          the question is: How do we go on? And even
more difficultly: What do you want? I've kissed women
          in cities to which I want never to return, but I would go there
          with you. I take too long to unpack my suitcase

every time I come home, until I need
          those socks again, until you can't stand

the sight of it, orange, leaning
          against the wall, full of patient fabric

                    and a foldable toothbrush. What do you want?
          How do you want me to give it
to you? The internet is full of stories today
          about boys playing Knockout, where they in passing

a stranger on the sidewalk, suddenly
                lash out with a blow to the back or front
        of the head. To enact upon the world
    such a specific report of the violence with which

it regularly seeks to kill you seems to me the opposite
                of senseless. It's time to eat
        the dictionary. All the newspapers

    moldering, unread. What do we mean
                when we talk about perfection?
        If I'd been better at life would we never
    have met? Here is the inventory. Here

                is the old lexicon, here all the things
    you left behind: Sorrow. Nevermind. Cardinal
                sleeping in throat chakra. Meditation cushion. One
        espresso maker, barely used. All the pots

    and pans. We can go get them. We can bring
                them here and eat in our pajamas and kiss in the kitchen
    and someday you will tell me the name you called yourself

    when you decided to leave that place. You will tell me
what the moon said, and the mirror
                the night you decided to come home.

    It's been a long century so far, full of clocks and obituaries
                and the law. The sight of your leather jacket
    emptied over the back of the rocking chair, how hot
                this tea is, the books in their authorial order—

comforts. If Camus was right, if speaking
                always involves a treason, every promise
    I can make you is less than this touch. Still, I think

our speaking redoes the world. So bring me
           your philosophies, the car radio, an extra
      set of house keys and the toy arrow

deconstructed on your studio floor.
Let's not leave this world in ruins.

white girl interrogates her own heart again

Shut the door. Outside, the newspapers fly themselves
against the stone and glass until the light stops. Come,
my little contradictory multi-chambered thudder.
Take the chair closest to the radiator. We love
our small comforts. Our lavender tea and quiet

boulevard. No one is blaming you
for these. Soldiers in all wars lean into
their vices, and I know that you hate war. But war
is here. Is you. Is our brilliant city, on fire even

as we speak. Is a flag we take to the back porch
to wring out softly, before family arrives.
So as not to discuss the blood. So as not
to discomfort those who made us. But heart, oh

heart. Discomfort is the weapon we bring to this
needful table. Without you, we are all statistic
or fist. Without you, more and more fire. Look
how the wind disturbs the curtains through
the closed window. Look how it finds a way in.

July, when we didn't burn the city down

Night after sorrow. Night without water
on its brow. Night crouched in the marrow
of park trees. City night. Swamp night.
Night without boots. Night the dead
watch arrive. Night the moon mothers
from a distance. Dozing lifeguard orchard
night. Night without protest. Yoked
night, night of the slack catapult. Night split
from the balm steeple and house
of hungry abundance. Night without
deliverance. Night without evidence.
Night of the rotten evidence alliance.
Night of derelict logic echoing
bones. Bone night. Night ground
to maggot powder. Night of the dull
knuckle blade, night of flamboyant
asphalt coagulation, red
night, night of the open shotgun
catalogue, of the too-small luggage
of language. Night
not everyone survives.

Not everyone survives.
Of language, night
catalogue of the too-small luggage
night, night of the open shotgun
asphalt coagulation, red
knuckle blade night. Of flamboyant
to maggot powder. Night of the dull
bones. Bone night. Night ground.
Night of derelict logic echoing.
Night of the rotten evidence alliance,
of hungry abundance. Night without,
from the balm steeple and house
night, night of the slack catapult. Night split
night. Night without protest. Yoked
from a distance. Dozing lifeguard orchard
watch arrive. Night the moon mothers,
night without boots. Night the dead
of park trees. City night. Swamp, night
on its brow. Night crouched in the marrow.
Night after sorrow. Night without water.

After sorrow. Without water
on its brow. In the marrow
of park trees. Without boots.
From a distance. Without protest
of the slack catapult
from the balm steeple
of hungry abundance. Without
deliverance. Without evidence.
Of the rotten evidence alliance,
of derelict logic. To maggot powder.
Of the dull, of flamboyant,
of the open shotgun
catalogue, of the too-small luggage
of language.

stars   linear   eternity? infinitude? loop?

cyclical   post-human   ?

moon   sky   suns   time   next   meteors   angels

moons

change   climate   sun   now   dinosaurs

clocks   pre   peri   post   giraffes

galaxy   planets   trees

universe   planet   apocalypse   beasts/monsters

machines   animals

technology   **Anthropocene**   humans   evolution

capitalism/consumerism   ocean   water

universes   gods/God   bodies   faces

consumption   salt   sleep   dreams

dreams   art

magic

hunger/thirst   love   sentence

connection   solitude

watershed

Salt dreams, and the memory of a single
horizon. Manatee lungs, the first girl
with gills. We were wrong about evolution.
Everything happens in at least two directions.

our joke

is that the end of days is just like
the beginning of days, but with more
plastic. Us and the giraffes, shockingly

strong swimmers, those reticulated
necks. What can we do but masturbate
and dream a life of constant increase?

The line of animal thoracic parting
the water, brief weeds mingling
in the wind—everything becomes sexual

when every touch is largely dust.
Here's the trick of being alive
in a dying time: there's never

any proof. *Animal, vegetable,*
mineral is now *rock, water,*
scissors. Now *milk, salt, milk.*

Still want that skin?

a thing

the movies got right: the prepared
fare no better than the foolish. It's all
as it was written, erased, traced over,
scribbled on by toddlers, and read aloud
in the bath. No apocalypse an end,
not even ours. Every moment, each
eyelash fall and atomic detonation one
flicker in this ball of stretched electric
light. Understand. My sisters and I used to take
the 8 mm films from our childhood
and run them backward. Birthday
presents re-wrapping their boxes,
milk re-filling the glass. Greedy magic.
Mom's hair braided, unbraided.
Braided, unbraided. Looking at us
now, looking away.

I mean

we've earned this extinction.
Another parasitic megafauna

on its way out the door.
Still, I like to look at you

and the water. I like to watch
the generator spark

and remember neon. That night
we sheltered in the car,

lightning all around us through
the trees, I said

it was not our end. And it wasn't,
and now I even miss

the sirens' wailing changing
nothing, hollering warning

across the dark unlistening water as if
we were not, even then, a mortuary shore.

honestly

I miss
the most
terribly small
domesticities: untangling
a delicate
necklace, picking
the metal knots out
with a pin. Scraping
the melted plastic
cutting board portions
off the metal arms
of the gas stove burner
cover. Vinegar
and a festering lemon
to trap those immortal
fruit flies. Here
in the now
where nothing
is as it was, or
easy, I bury my hands
in the hot earth, close
my eyes to the midnight
bright and think
Radiator. Teakettle.
Bathtub in a cool dark room.

not

that there's anything special about being
    alive, just that it's what we
    know. For all we know, what's next

        is spectacular in ways we can't in any way
        comprehend, or only get glimpses of

in recollected drawings of unicorns and other gods. I mean
    we don't even know what life
    is. A bag of water tied to a doorknob? A speaking

        creature let loose in a field? According to pretty much
        everything, the word

        for life is *more*. But more nothing
    is still nothing. That's what's at the bottom
            of the ocean. That's what the air's like here.

things we could be if we are not us

Maybe I'm a corridor, a coronary
bloodpath in some massive
gallivanting night-creature. And you're
the heartwall, the thudding
musculature right there, right there,
right there. Or a coniferous
tree, your hand
a taproot into irradiated
soil, my hair rising out into needles.
It would be night, and you
light on each teeming crest, me
the sucking trough drawing us back
into salt dark, forward to shore.

distance indicated by degrees of blue

I mean, we're here. Under this paling
chandelier of stars. All the moons
are out tonight, and you

have never been more beautiful.
Forget it all. This shadow
planet, our clockless

passage, the mirage of rapture.
We're waiting on nothing.
Nothing is our God

aperture, the gap by which
we know we exist, still, see
our fusing bodies

a titanium dialect make. A light
refuge. Watch the rapturous giraffes
maraud in the shallows.

We're too busy or far for God now.

in the dim,

quitted skinsuits—luminescent,
gutted—waltz in a concrete field.

Disputed code, what electronics
survive, high water, so much

digital and dried apparatus.
Negotiable as a sand labyrinth.

Symphonic thirst, a telescope
orchard, moored museum.

All the birds are gulls now
and female.

beloved

are you asking, is there any sweetness
left? Yesterday, I thought I saw
a bee. Instead, a tumble
of fur and snow. The light
jinxes knowing often now. I had
a bird, or it sang in the lilac
outside my curtains, or the hawk
dove to come up with a fish
striving its gills in the sudden air.
It was like this: bee, bird, lilac, snow,
air. And the ocean, which has
no sweetness in it. Ask me again
Is there any sweetness here? I will
say *Yes. Yes. My throat stumbles*
with honey when we sleep.

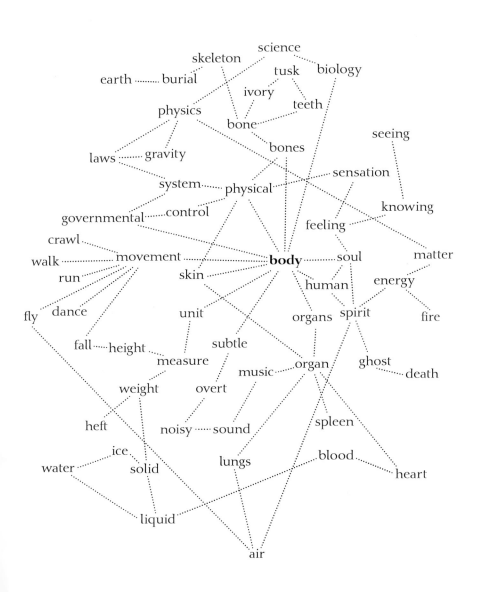

the sacrament of holding hands

How adults do not live: as chaos in the mouth
of winter. Eating organic but never sweeping the
floor. Unlicensed at the desk, stains on all the good
books, sunburned out of season. Nothing brings
us less pleasure than two dead Christmas trees on
the porch in February. We've tried so hard to be
brave, to live according to the real inside the skin
that ends our fingers and now here, this leafless
day, no drifts to pretty it, look at us. We're shining.
We may never die.

when they say you can't go home again, what they mean is you were never there

Maybe it's time to celebrate the hideous. Not
                    to confess with some hope for absolution,
          but to gather all the terrible selves and minutes
                    and show them the trees, and the way the rain

     has just abated so the air has ocean in it. Part of me died here
                    so another could go on walking the path on the hill
          where I became larger than myself and the day
                    could no longer contain me. Turns out, dust

          can also recompose itself, a starfish arm
     or lizard tail. What I cut off kept walking
                    without me, remembering the fireflies
          on the broad lawn and plastic cups

          in dormitory basements, the tea house
     and everything I shamelessly left in pursuit of the shining
                    next. I'm saying I've learned to breathe
          as if I were always

          singing. I wish I could say everything I've done
     and still be loved. I feel
                    this enormous debt to the world
          for letting me exist and do all the damage

                    my living requires. I'm hungry
     and the tea is cold, the hill is a hill
     no matter who I am. It will take a long time
                    to say the everything, and already

          some are turning away. It's hard
     work, witnessing at a birth. Blood
          everywhere, and the awful quiet
     between the screaming. You can bring

your everything too, we're making
the dirt arable again. We're burying
        our shit like animals do and tomorrow
there will be a garden ringed

with lemon trees though by then
        we'll be on our way gone. For luck,
                afterbirth under the single poplar.
                        All the stopping and starting, interruptions

        of prayer. Language as vehicle
                        and impediment. All the lives
before this one, practice. Is that a castle
        in your elbow? My clavicle's made

        of mud. I'm trying to tell you
                        about my fear. A door opening
        in another room. The way light changes
                after rain, the air around a body

        after sweat. I'm not
                        finished yet. Somebody
kiss me now, right on the garden.
                Everything's coming up green.

disasterology: how to survive the apocalypse

Every day I become the horizon. Don't you? The way
the sky eats itself, in fire or fog. I want to fold down

into a nothing you can't forget, smoke in the air
long after the fire's gone, molecules

next to molecules. We're neighbors, you and I. You
and the wind. I and the horizon, where it bends

into an envelope. I've said this before.
Were you listening? The thickness of the air

affects how well sound travels. I don't hear
very well around corners, though I can tell

when a machine has been left on in a room
from outside a closed door. I need you to hear this.

I turned off the radio because I lost count
of the dying. But if you are the sky. And I

am the sky. And nothing but atoms
between us, nothing but smoke or the memory

of smoke, its scent in pieces
in the air. If distance is a myth and we

are neighbors, or the same creature with multiple
faces, breathing the common, unspeakable air

which has us in pieces, I'm nothing
without you. Don't say it's too late to try.

how

The tree shadows make a ladder
of the road, or a bar code.

I could bring this fallen bark
inside, dry it until the bugs
run out, call it art.

Yellow chair, wind chime,
tree swing, yard violet,
telephone wire.

Cardinals in the fir tree,
wings mimicking flapping fabric
drying on the line—

a sound I haven't heard in years.

actual rapture

Day with rejoicing. Day with the wind
in its shoes. Day splintering winter
behind the heels of joggers.
Day with seeds. Day without rot.
Day hungry for lemons. Day starved
for bright. Day thirsty for reservoir hips.
Day reservoir for sorrow. Day hold sorrow
like a grandfather's basement grenade. Willow-
scaling day. Wave-chasing day. Day
even the moon can't abandon. Day tuned
to the samurai channel. Day the mushrooms
bloom. Cicada-hum day. Comet-miss-us
day. Day of automatic altars. Day we tip
our faces up to swallow clouds.
Day we become our own species.
Day we assume the posture of funk
and play the banjo loud. Day we shutter
the homicide shop and museum
the epileptic streets. Day worth its weight
in pigment and ash. Blue day. Blues day.
Day invented testimony. Day bastard chapel.
Day mystic hymns. Day rivet the buildings. Day
map the hood. Day weave no memory shroud. Day
cover no forever face. Day put no pennies
on no eyes in no fountains day of no wishes
only spells. Day with no shouting. Day with no fire.
Bright-lensed day. Day built for singing. Day
nobody dies. Day nobody dies.

acknowledgments

First gratitude goes to Lindsey, who inspires and draws me into larger and larger life every day. I love you, more and more.

Infinite gratitude to Phillip B. Williams, Maya Marshall, and Ben Clark for your brilliant edits, bright patience, and confidence that this book could both make its own world and find its way in this one.

Thank you to Hedgebrook for the space and time needed to make room for the productive madness required for poetry, and for the snacks needed to survive it.

Thanks to the Vox Ferus community for keeping me tethered to the poetry realm, for your vulnerability and trust and wine.

The circle that holds and grounds me: Mariah, Stacy, Kim, Missy, Emily Rose, Miquela.

Mom and Dad, Erin and Kristin, since forever and for always. The Niro and Falknor clans, for always.

•

"actual rapture" appeared in *The Massachusetts Review*, Winter 2017.

"the admiral" appeared in *Jet Fuel Review*, Fall 2013.

"distance indicated by degrees of blue" appeared in *The Gettysburg Review*, Spring 2017, as "agnostic seduction post-apoc."

"elegy instructions" appeared in *Court Green*, January 2015, as "another elegy."

"February" appeared in *Tahoma Literary Review*, December 2014.

"fuse" appeared in the anthology *For Some Time Now: Performance Poets of New York City*, August 2012.

"Isla Vista" appeared in *Bone Bouquet*, Summer 2017.

"July, when we didn't burn the city down" appeared in *Pamplemousse*, Winter 2017.

"lucky" appeared in *CALYX*, Winter/Spring 2017, as "for the last dude who asked why I'm so angry."

"not" appeared in *Southern Indiana Review*, Fall 2018.

"notes on the warranted strife to come" appeared in *Vinyl*, February 2016.

"queerer weather" appeared in *The Nervous Breakdown*, September 2015.

"radio silence, WENZ, WJMO, Cleveland" appeared in *Poetry Northwest*, Summer 2017.

"the reckoning" appeared in *Pamplemousse*, Winter 2017.

"the sacrament of holding hands" appeared in *The Gettysburg Review*, Spring 2017.

"the sacrament of penance also has four parts" appeared in *The Massachusetts Review*, Winter 2017.

"supplication with grimy windowpane" appeared in *Columbia Poetry Review*, Spring 2015.

"treatise on the nature of non-abandonment" appeared in *Breakwater Review*, December 2015.

"West Barry Street" appeared in *LEVELER*, February 23, 2014.

"when the time comes to be happy, you will be happy" appeared in *Pamplemousse* online, February 2017.

"when they say you can't go home again, what they mean is you were never there" appeared in *The Adroit Journal*, Summer 2016.

"white girl interrogates her own heart again" appeared in *Compose*, Spring 2016.

"white girl interrogates her recurring dreams" appeared in *Southern Indiana Review*, Fall 2018.

"white girl interrogates her unreliable memory of certain eras" appeared in *Southern Indiana Review*, Fall 2018.

Marty McConnell is the author of *wine for a shotgun* (EM Press, 2013) and *Gathering Voices: Creating a Community-Based Poetry Workshop* (YesYes Books, 2018). She is the co-creator of *underbelly*, an online magazine focused on the art and magic of poetry revision. An MFA graduate of Sarah Lawrence College, her work has appeared in numerous journals and anthologies including *Best American Poetry*, *The Gettysburg Review*, *Gulf Coast*, and *Indiana Review*. She lives in Chicago with her wife, visual artist Lindsey Dorr-Niro.

The Michael Waters Poetry Prize was established in 2013 to honor Michael's contributions to *Southern Indiana Review* and American arts and letters.

MWPP Winners

2017—Marty McConnell

2016—Ruth Awad

2015—Annie Kim

2014—Dennis Hinrichsen & Hannah Faith Notess

2013—Doug Ramspeck

Southern
Indiana
Review
Press